Presented to: _____

From: _____

*Your word is a lamp to my feet
and a light for my path.*

—Psalm 119:105

Bible Promises for Students
Copyright 1998 Zondervan Corporation
ISBN 0-310-97690-1

Excerpts taken from:
The New Student Bible, New International Version
Copyright 1986, 1992 by The Zondervan Corporation
The Holy Bible: New International Version (North American Edition). Copyright 1973, 1978, 1984 by International Bible Society. Used by permission of Zondervan Publishing House. All rights reserved.

Requests for information should be addressed to:

ZondervanPublishingHouse
Mail Drop B20
Grand Rapids, Michigan 49530
http://www.zondervan.com

Senior Editor: Gwen Ellis
Compilers: Candy Paull and Molly Detweiler
Design: Mark Veldheer

Printed in the United States of America
98   99   00   01 /DP/ 3   2   1

Trust in the LORD with all your heart and lean not on your own understanding; in all your ways acknowledge him, and he will make your paths straight.

PROVERBS 3:5–6

Do not let this Book of the Law depart from your mouth; meditate on it day and night, so that you may be careful to do everything written in it.

JOSHUA 1:8

In the original Hebrew, "in all your ways acknowledge him" is more literally "in all your ways know him." Nodding in God's direction is not enough: you must know him by living closely with him, relating to him personally in every aspect of your life.

*T*rust in the LORD forever,
for the LORD, the LORD
is the Rock eternal.

ISAIAH 26:4

Isaiah, who lived in a time of tremendous turmoil, urged believers to focus on a reality greater than their current troubles: to keep their minds steady on God, who never loses control over events.

*T*he Word became flesh and made his dwelling among us. We have seen his glory, the glory of the One and Only, who came from the Father, full of grace and truth.

JOHN 1:14

You were valuable enough to God that he was willing to give the life of his only Son. God loved you so much that he freely gave his only Son so that you might have eternal life. That's how much he valued your life.

*For you created my inmost being . . .
I praise you because I am fearfully
and wonderfully made.*

PSALM 139:13–14

When does life begin? God's loving involvement with our lives starts long before birth. Nothing can escape God's concern— no person, no thought, no place, no time.

I am with you and will watch over you wherever you go . . . I will not leave you until I have done what I have promised you."

GENESIS 28:15

Some things are beyond understanding.
We can only fall back on this simple advice:
fear God and obey him, no matter how
things seem to us. Live a life of faith.

How ow beautiful on the mountains are the feet of those who bring good news, who proclaim peace, who bring good tidings, who proclaim salvation, who say . . . "Your God reigns!"

ISAIAH 52:7

Isaiah portrays the joy of carrying good news to those desperately hoping for it—perhaps a city waiting for news of a battle in which all their young men were at risk. But Isaiah's news is not of war; it is of God's people returning from exile, with the LORD himself leading the way.

*T*he LORD, the LORD, the compassionate and gracious God, slow to anger, abounding in love and faithfulness, maintaining love to thousands, and forgiving wickedness, rebellion and sin.

EXODUS 34:6–7

Above all, love each other deeply, because love covers over a multitude of sins.

1 PETER 4:8

Let us hold unswervingly to the hope we profess, for he who promised is faithful.

HEBREWS 10:23

In the book of Isaiah a devastating chapter on God's judgment of the whole earth is followed with a bright promise of a future life. Then, death and pain will be abolished, and God will reign with perfect peace.

*T*he LORD *their God will save them on that day as the flock of his people. They will sparkle in his land like jewels in a crown.*

ZECHARIAH 9:16

Picture God as a master jeweler and yourself as a priceless diamond in the rough. Paul probably had something like that in mind when he wrote, "We are God's workmanship." We are his workmanship, but as yet we're uncompleted projects. So be patient.

But in keeping with his promise we are looking forward to a new heaven and a new earth, the home of righteousness.

2 PETER 3:13

The Bible never ignores the emotions of the moment. But the Bible also insists on a long-range perspective. Difficulties won't last; God's care does.

I urge ... that requests, prayers, intercession and thanksgiving be made for everyone—for ... all those in authority, that we may live peaceful and quiet lives in all godliness and holiness.

1 TIMOTHY 2:1–2

Paul lays decision-making out almost like a formula. I can know God's will for my life if I give God: my body as a living sacrifice; my will by letting him control my life; my mind by keeping it pure and flooding it with his Word.

The LORD delights in those who fear him, who put their hope in his unfailing love.

PSALM 147:11

The LORD is a God of strength . . . but power doesn't delight him. More than anything he loves to be in a close relationship to people who respond to his love.

*How can a young man keep
his way pure? By living according
to your word.*

∽

PSALM 119:9

In Deuteronomy the author portrays God as a father with his children, as a mother who gives them life, as an eagle hovering over its young. In return, God asks for obedience based on love.

Better a poor but wise youth than an old but foolish king who no longer knows how to take warning.

ECCLESIASTES 4:13

Old Testament writers made clear that God really wanted obedient lives, not ritual performances. Only Jesus' sacrifice has the power to actually forgive sins and change lives.

*R*emember this: Whoever sows sparingly will also reap sparingly, and whoever sows generously will also reap generously.

2 CORINTHIANS 9:6

Giving actually enriches and benefits the giver, the apostle Paul says in 2 Corinthians. Also, a gift can serve as an act of worship to God and can inspire other people's faith and thanksgiving.

"We tell you the good news: What God promised our fathers he has fulfilled for us, their children, by raising up Jesus."

⌒

ACTS 13:32–33

People often try to bargain with God, thinking that by their good deeds they can get God to do what they want. But God is rich beyond our dreams; he has no need of our offerings. What matters to him is the attitude we take toward him.

But now he has appeared once for all at the end of the ages to do away with sin by the sacrifice of himself.

HEBREWS 9:26

Step by step, the author of Hebrews shows how Christ's new covenant improves on the old one. Instead of many sacrifices, he made only one, himself, thus gaining free and complete forgiveness for us.

As you come to him, the living Stone—rejected by men but chosen by God and precious to him—you also, like living stones, are being built into a spiritual house to be a holy priesthood.

1 PETER 2:4–5

The Creator of the Universe paid the highest price that can be paid to give you the chance to experience a personal relationship with God through Jesus Christ, to be totally forgiven of your sins, and to live forever.
You are priceless.

Who is a God like you, who pardons sin and forgives the transgression of the remnant of his inheritance? You do not stay angry forever but delight to show mercy.

MICAH 7:18

Theologians use big words to describe God's unique qualities: transcendence, omnipotence, omnipresence. The prophet Micah marveled even more over this: God's forgiveness.

Since my youth, O God, you have taught me, and to this day I declare your marvelous deeds.

PSALM 71:17

By God's standards for our lives, we all fall short. But we're assured in Philippians 2:13 that we're not struggling alone. God is at work in us to *help* us desire and attain his standard and purpose for our lives.

*B*lessed is the man who perseveres under trial, because when he has stood the test, he will receive the crown of life that God has promised to those who love him.

JAMES 1:12

In the "fight of the faith," the odds sometimes seem staggering. Yet the Bible indicates an eternal prize awaits those who remain faithful to the final bell.

*Return to the LORD your God, for
he is gracious and compassionate, slow
to anger and abounding in love, and
he relents from sending calamity.*

JOEL 2:13

Be aware of God's presence; talk to him all day long. If you could see Jesus by your side all day, you would talk to him constantly. Well, he's really there—and he would like to talk with you.

May the LORD, the God
of your fathers, . . . bless you
as he has promised!

DEUTERONOMY 1:11

The LORD your God is with you, he is mighty to save. He will take great delight in you, he will quiet you with his love, he will rejoice over you with singing.

ZEPHANIAH 3:17

Let the rivers clap their hands, let the mountains sing together for joy; let them sing before the LORD, for he comes to judge the earth.

PSALM 98:8–9

God's salvation doesn't just affect human beings. When rebellion against God finally ends, nature itself will celebrate.

May our Lord Jesus Christ himself and God our Father, who loved us and by his grace gave us eternal encouragement and good hope, encourage your hearts and strengthen you in every good deed and word.

2 THESSALONIANS 2:16–17

Let us consider how we may spur one another on toward love and good deeds. Let us not give up meeting together, as some are in the habit of doing, but let us encourage one another—and all the more as you see the Day approaching.

HEBREWS 10:24–25

When I said, "My foot is slipping,"
your love, O LORD, supported me.

PSALM 94:18

In James 4:8 the Bible says, "Come near to God and he will come near to you." It's a great relief to sense God's presence. He wants to be the still point of your turning, twisting, ever-changing world.

*T*herefore, if anyone is in Christ, he is a new creation; the old has gone, the new has come!

2 CORINTHIANS 5:17

For God who said, "Let light shine out of darkness," made his light shine in our hearts to give us the light of the knowledge of the glory of God in the face of Christ.

2 CORINTHIANS 4:6

But we have this treasure in jars of clay to show that this all-surpassing power is from God and not from us.

2 Corinthians 4:7

The treasure Paul refers to in 2 Corinthians 4:7 is the incredible message of the gospel: God's good news of forgiveness and the promise of life forever. An immortal God chooses mere humans as his personal representatives.

You are a gracious and compassionate God, slow to anger and abounding in love, a God who relents from sending calamity.

JONAH 4:2

The poet Robert Frost said, "After Jonah, you could never trust God not to be merciful again." Pointedly, the book of Jonah ends with a question. Can anyone put limits on God's mercy and forgiveness?

If we confess our sins, he is faithful and just and will forgive us our sins and purify us from all unrighteousness.

1 JOHN 1:9

In the Bible, love is more than a feeling; it is a decision to serve another person's interest. Only through God's help can this decision be made with "all your heart."

God is not a man, that he should lie, nor a son of man, that he should change his mind. Does he speak and then not act? Does he promise and not fulfill?

*J*esus said, "Everything is possible for him who believes."

MARK 9:23

"The LORD himself goes before you and will be with you; he will never leave you nor forsake you. Do not be afraid; do not be discouraged."

DEUTERONOMY 31:8

This world may be full of pollution, war, crime and hate. But inside all of us linger remnants that remind us of what the world could be like. That perfect world is not merely a dream; it will come true (see the last few chapters of Revelation).

The LORD *will guide you always.*

ISAIAH 58:11

*F*lee the evil desires of youth, and pursue righteousness, faith, love and peace, along with those who call on the Lord out of a pure heart.

2 TIMOTHY 2:22

*L*et us then approach the throne of grace with confidence, so that we may receive mercy and find grace to help us in our time of need.

HEBREWS 4:16

"Though the mountains be shaken and the hills be removed, yet my unfailing love for you will not be shaken nor my covenant of peace be removed," says the LORD, who has compassion on you.

Isaiah 54:10

"*Come to me, all you who are weary and burdened, and I will give you rest.*"

MATTHEW 11:28

God works patiently. He doesn't spot something negative in your life and then twist your arm until you make it right. He loves you until you, of your own free will, decide you want what he wants.

We also rejoice in our sufferings, because we know that suffering produces perseverance; perseverance, character; and character, hope. And hope does not disappoint us, because God has poured out his love into our hearts by the Holy Spirit, whom he has given us.

ROMANS 5:3–5

Just as God hasn't given up on you, so you shouldn't give up on others who also are God's workmanship. Knowing how patient God has been with you should help you demonstrate patience toward others.

*For you have been my hope,
O Sovereign LORD, my confidence
since my youth.*

PSALM 71:5

Joyce Huggett notes the importance of understanding how much God loves you: "If you know yourself to be deeply loved by someone who will never let you down, fail you, or phase out of your life, you are rich in resources."

You will know that I am the LORD; those who hope in me will not be disappointed."

ISAIAH 49:23

*F*ind rest, O my soul, in God alone; my hope comes from him. He alone is my rock and my salvation; he is my fortress, I will not be shaken.

PSALM 62:5–6

But may the righteous be glad and rejoice before God; may they be happy and joyful.

PSALM 68:3

The word *wisdom* brings up pictures of gray-haired old men muttering obscure philosophic maxims. But wisdom is above all practical and down-to-earth. Becoming wise requires self-discipline to study and humbly seek wisdom at every opportunity.

Don't let anyone look down on you because you are young, but set an example for the believers in speech, in life, in love, in faith and in purity.

1 TIMOTHY 4:12

A full-time Christian is someone who realizes that his or her relationship with Jesus is the most important thing in life. A full-time Christian is someone who's willing to let God use him or her any way he sees fit.

Even youths grow tired and weary, and young men stumble and fall; but those who hope in the LORD will renew their strength. They will soar on wings like eagles; they will run and not grow weary, they will walk and not be faint.

ISAIAH 40:30–31

How can we overcome temptation? *Answer:* By following the example of Jesus. Led into the wilderness, Christ resisted enticements to sin by quoting Scripture. So memorize a couple of verses today that deal with specific temptations you face.

Be happy, young man, while you are young, and let your heart give you joy in the days of your youth.

ECCLESIASTES 11:9

The first recorded covenant God made with us was marked by an appropriate symbol—the rainbow. While later covenants applied specifically to the Israelites, this one extended—and still extends— to every living creature.

Your promises have been thoroughly tested, and your servant loves them.

PSALM 119:140

The LORD is my rock, my fortress and my deliverer; my God is my rock, in whom I take refuge. He is my shield and the horn of my salvation, my stronghold.

PSALM 18:2

*T*he joy of the LORD *is your strength.*

NEHEMIAH 8:10

Jesus said, "Are not five sparrows sold for two pennies? Yet not one of them is forgotten by God. Don't be afraid; you are worth more than many sparrows."

LUKE 12:6–7

For I am convinced that neither death nor life, neither angels nor demons, neither the present nor the future, nor any powers, neither height nor depth, nor anything else in all creation, will be able to separate us from the love of God that is in Christ Jesus our Lord.

ROMANS 8:38–39

Prayer is a conversation between two people who love each other. But it won't be much of a conversation if you don't *talk* to him about your hopes and dreams and fears and disappointments. He wants to hear your expressions of love and your thanks.

Therefore I will praise you among the nations, O LORD; I will sing praises to your name.

PSALM 18:49

*I will lie down and sleep
in peace, for you alone, O LORD,
make me dwell in safety.*

PSALM 4:8

Jesus said, "Surely I am with you always, to the very end of the age."

∽

MATTHEW 28:20

Love is not just another mark of a Christian, but the *birthmark* of a Christian. In other words, your life as a Christian should be marked first by your love for God, and then by your love for others.

*B*e still before the LORD and
wait patiently for him. . . .

PSALM 37:7

Keep your eyes open for people of integrity. When you find someone who tells the truth, keeps his or her promises, and takes responsibility for his or her behavior . . . latch onto that person!

*Love is patient, love is kind. It does not envy,
it does not boast, it is not proud. It is not rude,
it is not self-seeking, it is not easily angered,
it keeps no record of wrongs.*

1 CORINTHIANS 13:4–5

There is no fear in love.
But perfect love drives out fear.

1 JOHN 4:18

Do not be anxious about anything, but in everything, by prayer and petition, with thanksgiving, present your requests to God. And the peace of God, which transcends all understanding, will guard your hearts and your minds in Christ Jesus.

PHILIPPIANS 4:6–7

*C*ast all your anxiety on him
because he cares for you.

1 PETER 5:7

The LORD bless you and keep you;
the LORD make his face shine upon you
and be gracious to you; the LORD turn his
face toward you and give you peace.

NUMBERS 6:24–26

He who began a good work in
you will carry it on to completion
until the day of Christ Jesus.

PHILIPPIANS 1:6

*F*or God so loved the world that he gave his one and only Son, that whoever believes in him shall not perish but have eternal life.

JOHN 3:16

John 3:16 has probably been memorized more than any other verse in the Bible. In a few words it tells the story of salvation: God's love for the world, God's gift of his Son, and the opportunity for anyone who believes to be saved.

Teach me your way, O LORD, and I will walk in your truth; give me an undivided heart, that I may fear your name.

PSALM 86:11

David prayed for an undivided heart, in order to give all of it to God in his praise. "Heart" in the Bible doesn't refer to emotions, but to the whole person. David's prayer meant, "Help me aim myself in a single direction!"

The LORD *gives strength
to his people; the* LORD *blesses
his people with peace.*

PSALM 29:11

People respond to guilt in different ways. Our response can either drive us farther from God or closer to him. God only asks that we admit our need and trust him. And then we can walk in newness of life—precious, free, forgiven life.

"I have told you these things, so that in me you may have peace. In this world you will have trouble. But take heart! I have overcome the world."

JOHN 16:33

*B*ecause of the LORD's great love we are not consumed, for his compassions never fail. They are new every morning; great is your faithfulness.

LAMENTATIONS 3:22–23

Mercy, peace and love be
yours in abundance.

JUDE 1:2

*J*esus said, "I am the resurrection and the life. He who believes in me will live, even though he dies; and whoever lives and believes in me will never die."

JOHN 11:25–26

*You will keep in perfect peace
him whose mind is steadfast, because
he trusts in you.*

ISAIAH 26:3

God accepted Abraham not because he led a perfect life but because of his responsiveness to God's promises. Even in the Old Testament, God looked for faith, not moral perfection.

*Delight yourself in the
LORD and he will give you the
desires of your heart.*

PSALM 37:4

If you feel discouraged or wonder if God really cares or question whether the Christian life is worth the effort, read Ephesians. You will no longer feel like an orphan.

*B*e joyful always; pray continually; give thanks in all circumstances, for this is God's will for you in Christ Jesus.

1 THESSALONIANS 5:16–18

The best way to figure out what Jesus would want you to do is to look at how he made decisions. Because of his close, moment-by-moment relationship to his heavenly Father, Jesus made the right choices.

Jesus said, "Do not let your hearts be troubled. Trust in God; trust also in me."

JOHN 14:1

*The Spirit of Truth . . . will guide
you into all truth.*

JOHN 16:13

For it is God who works in you to will and to act according to his good purpose.

PHILIPPIANS 2:13

You can easily become obsessed with other people's wrongs against you. But you can also turn your thoughts to God and quiet your anxieties while strengthening your commitment.

*P*lace me like a seal over your heart, like a seal on your arm; for love is as strong as death, its jealousy unyielding as the grave.

SONG OF SONGS 8:6

Love: it takes control of your life, and like a gigantic fire, it cannot be doused. Love must be treated with the greatest caution and respect.

"*I have loved you with an everlasting love; I have drawn you with loving-kindness.*"

JEREMIAH 31:3

You are a chosen people, a royal priesthood, a holy nation, a people belonging to God, that you may declare the praises of him who called you out of darkness into his wonderful light.

1 PETER 2:9

*F*or it is by grace you have been saved, through faith—and this not from yourselves, it is the gift of God—not by works, so that no one can boast.

EPHESIANS 2:8–9

Paul insisted on one fact of the gospel: eternal life comes not by any ritual of rule-keeping, but by the grace of God. Yet he notes that God intends for us to "do good works."

The law of the LORD is perfect, reviving the soul. The statutes of the LORD are trustworthy, making wise the simple.

PSALM 19:7

*You were once darkness,
but now you are light in the Lord.
Live as children of light.*

EPHESIANS 5:8

*A*nd we know that in all things God works for the good of those who love him, who have been called according to his purpose.

ROMANS 8:28

God has promised to meet our needs. "And my God will meet all your needs according to his glorious riches in Christ Jesus," the Bible says in Philippians 4:19. We can believe that he will—and relax.

"*Fear not, for I have redeemed you;*
I have summoned you by name; you are mine.
You are precious and honored in my sight,
and ... I love you."

ISAIAH 43:1,4

Have I not commanded you? Be strong and courageous. Do not be terrified; do not be discouraged, for the LORD your God will be with you wherever you go.

JOSHUA 1:9

Taste and see that the LORD is good;
blessed is the man who takes refuge in him.
Fear the LORD, you his saints, for those
who fear him lack nothing.

PSALM 34:8–9

If God is for us, who can be against us?
He who did not spare his own Son, but gave him
up for us all—how will he not also, along with
him, graciously give us all things?

ROMANS 8:31–32

*Blessed are those who hunger and thirst for
righteousness, for they will be filled.*

MATTHEW 5:6

Human beings have always longed for a perfect world. Isaiah repeatedly promises just that. The key to that new era will be an intimate relationship with God. "Before they call I will answer; while they are still speaking I will hear."

"You will seek me and find me when you seek me with all your heart. I will be found by you," declares the LORD.

JEREMIAH 29:13–14

As on Wall Street, "survival of the fittest" might have been Jerusalem's motto. Its officials were like wolves, devouring everything in sight. Could only the ruthless survive? Yet Jesus said, "Blessed are the meek, for they will inherit the earth" (Matthew 5:5).

I know that my Redeemer
lives, and that in the end he
will stand upon the earth.

JOB 19:25

Psalm 102:26 predicts that the universe, which God made, will wear out like old clothes. But God remains the same forever—and he will preserve his people, whom he is committed to far more than to his universe.

Surely God is my salvation; I will trust and not be afraid. The LORD, the LORD, is my strength and my song; he has become my salvation.

ISAIAH 12:2

I can do everything through [Christ] who gives me strength.

PHILIPPIANS 4:13

I have no greater joy than to hear that my children are walking in the truth.

3 JOHN 4

To see God's face is to see and know him personally, deeply, and without the clouds of mystery that so often make faith difficult.

*A*ll Scripture is God-breathed and is useful for teaching, rebuking, correcting and training in righteousness.

2 TIMOTHY 3:16

We do not know what we ought to pray for, but the Spirit himself intercedes for us with groans that words cannot express.

ROMANS 8:26

*"But blessed is the man
who trusts in the LORD, whose
confidence is in him."*

JEREMIAH 17:7

*J*esus replied, "I will do whatever you ask in my name, so that the Son may bring glory to the Father. You may ask me for anything in my name, and I will do it."

JOHN 14:13–14

If any of you lacks wisdom, he should ask God, who gives generously to all without finding fault, and it will be given to him.

JAMES 1:5

Guide me in your truth and teach me, for you are God my Savior, and my hope is in you all day long.

PSALM 25:5

Let the morning bring me word of your unfailing love, for I have put my trust in you. Show me the way I should go, for to you I lift up my soul.

PSALM 143:8

God's law liberates by freeing us from the destructive impact of sinful behavior. Only by following God's commands can a person escape the frustrating sense of boundaries.

He makes me lie down in green pastures, he leads me beside quiet waters, he restores my soul.

PSALM 23:2–3

The "apple of your eye" is an Old English expression for the eye's center, or pupil. The whole body is tuned to protect that pupil from harm. Proverbs urges you to take as much care of its teachings as you do of your eye.

*Commit to the LORD whatever you do,
and your plans will succeed.*

PROVERBS 16:3